EŞU — ELEGBA

IFÁ AND THE DIVINE MESSENGER

AWO FÁ'LOKUN FATUNMBI
OMO AWO FATUNMISE, ILE IFE,
BABALAWO ÈGBÈ IFÁ, ODE REMO,
OLUWO ILẸ̀ ÒRÚNMÌLÁ OSHUN, OAKLAND, CA

ESU-ELEGBA; Ifa and the Divine Messenger
By Awo Fa'lokun Fatunmbi

ISBN: 0-942272-27-7

Original Publications
P.O. Box 236
Old Bethpage, New York 11804-0236
(888) OCCULT-1

www.OCCULT1.com

Printed in the United States of America

ACKNOWLEDGEMENTS

The material in this book is primarily based on oral instruction from the elders of *Ifá* in Ode Remo, Ogun State Nigeria and Ile Ife, Oshun State Nigeria. In appreciation for their time, patience and loving concern for my training and spiritual guidance I say; *A dúpé Ègbè Ifá Ode Remo, Babalawo* Adesanya Awoyade, *Babalawo* Babalola Akinsanya, *Babalawo* Saibu Lamiyo, *Babalawo* Odujosi Awoyade, *Babalawo* Olu Taylor, *Babalawo* Abokede Aralbadan, *Babalawo* Biodun Debona, *Babalawo* Oluwasina Kuti, *Babalawo* Afolabi Kuti, *Babalawo* Fagbemi Fasina, *Babalawo* Oropotoniyan and all the members of Ègbè Apetebi Ode Remo.

A dúpé Awon Ifá Fatunmise Ègbè Ifá Ile Ifé, Jolofinpe Falaju Fatunmise, *Babalawo* Ganiyu Olaifa Fatunmise, *Babalawo* Awoleke Awofisan Lokore, *Babalawo* Ifaioye Fatunmise, *Babalawo* Ifanimowu Fatunmise, *Babalawo* Ifasure Fatunmise *Babalawo* Adebolu Fatunmise and all the members of *Egbe Apetebi Awon Fatunmise*.

A special thank you to the members of *Ilé Òrúnmìlà Oshun* for their continuing support and understanding, *Olori Yeye Aworo Timilade Apetebi Orunmila Iya l'Orisha Oshun Miwa* (Luisah Teish), *Eko'fa Iya lorisha Omijinka, Iya l'Orisha Iya Oshun Iya Osogbo, Iya l'Orisha Shango Wenwa,* Leona Jacobs-White, Nzinga Denny, Earthea Nance, Vance Williams, Blackberri, Salim Abdul-Jelani, Rebecca Schiros, Carol Lanigan, Zena Attig, T'hisha, Rose Sand, Xochipala MaesValdez, Dee Orr, Nina Haft and Hinton Jemoke.

A final thank you to Maureen Pattarelli for her work in editing this manuscript.

A dúpé okuku su wi awo aganjo, I thank all those who greet the Mysteries of Creation.

Awo Fá'lokun Fatunmbi
Oakland, CA

Eşu Yangi, The Divine Messenger at the Crossroads

TABLE OF CONTENTS

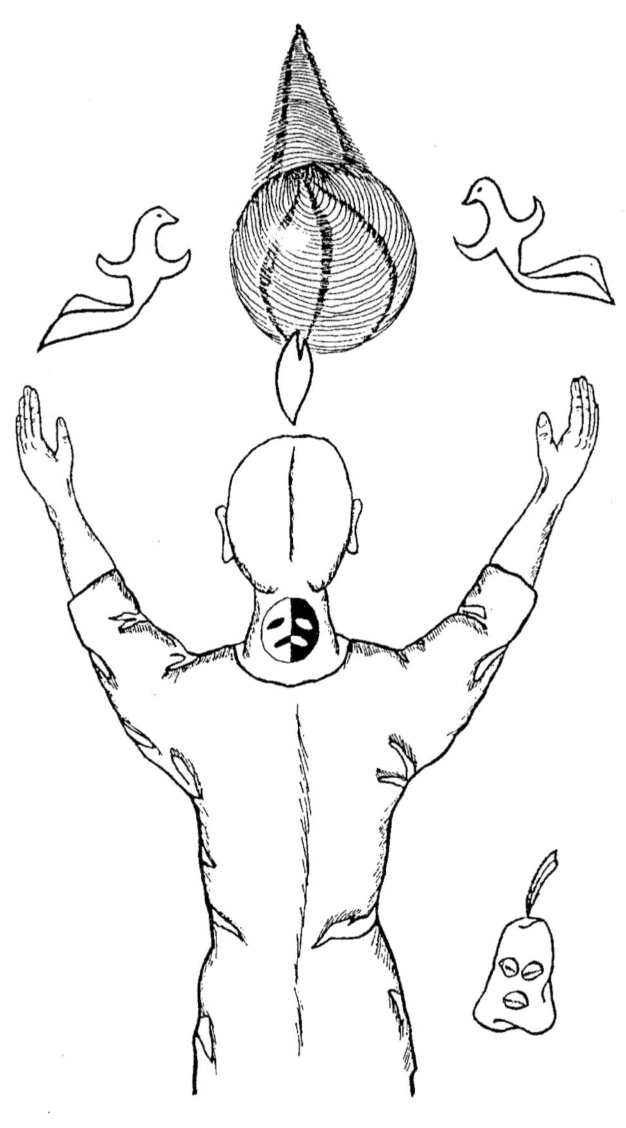

Eşu ni bako, The Divine Messenger is a Trickster

INTRODUCTION

Eşu is the Divine Messenger of the West African religious tradition called "*Ifá*".

The word *Eşu* is the name given to describe a complex convergence of Spiritual Forces that are at the foundation of *Ifá* cosmology. There is no literal translation for the word *Ifá*, it refers to a religious tradition, an understanding of ethics, a process of spiritual transformation and a set of scriptures that are the basis for a complex system of divination.

Ifá is found throughout the African diaspora where it spread as an integral part of Yoruba culture. The Yoruba Nation is located in the south western region of Nigeria. Prior to colonization, the Yoruba Nation was a federation of city states that was originally centered in the city of *Ilẹ̀ Ifẹ*. According to *Ifá* myth, the Yorubas migrated to *Ilẹ̀ Ifẹ* from the east under the leadership of a warrior chief named *Oduduwa*. It is difficult to date the time of the Yoruba move into West Africa because of limited archaeological research on the subject. Estimates range from between sixteen hundred to twenty-five hundred years ago. It is likely that migration took place over a number of generations. As the population grew, each new city state that became a part of the Yoruba federation was governed by a chief called "*Oba*". The position of *Oba* is a form of hereditary monarchy and each *Oba* goes through an initiation that makes them a spiritual descendant of *Oduduwa*.

Traditional Yoruba political institutions are very much integrated with traditional Yoruba religious institutions. Both structures survived British rule in Nigeria, and continue to function alongside the current civil government.

Within the discipline of *Ifá*, there is a body of wisdom called "*awo*," which attempts to preserve the rituals that create direct communication with Forces in Nature. *Awo* is a Yoruba word that is usually translated to mean "secret". Unfortunately, there is no real English equivalent to the word *awo*, because the word carries strong cultural and esoteric associations. In traditional Yoruba culture, *awo* refers to the hidden principles that explain the Mystery of Creation and Evolution. *Awo* is the esoteric understanding of the invisible forces that sustain dynamics and form within Nature. The essence of these invisible forces are not considered secret because they are devious, they are secret because they remain elusive, awesome in their power to transform and not readily apparent. As such they can only be grasped through direct interaction and participation. Anything which can be known by the intellect alone ceases to be *awo*.

The primal inspiration for *awo* is the communication between transcendent Spiritual Forces and human consciousness. This communication is believed to be facilitated by the Spirit of *Eşu*. Within the *awo* of *Ifá, Eşu* is described as having twenty-one different aspects or roads. In simple terms, this suggests that the ability to communicate with Spiritual Forces has a variety of distinct characteristics. Each of these characteristics has a very specific function within the framework of *Ifá* ritual.

Eşu is referred to as the Divine Messenger because of the key function of *Eşu* in *Ifá* ritual. Some Yoruba-English dictionaries and some anthropological manuscripts translate *Eşu* to mean "Devil". This translation is not consistent with the description of *Eşu* in *Ifá* scripture. *Eşu* can take the role of a trickster, but this role has the function of transforming deceptive and limited visions of self and world. It is the role of the trickster in all earth-centered religions to shake loose the limited perceptions that cause stagnation rather than growth. Only those who believe that they are in possession of the "Absolute Truth" view the trickster as a "demonic spirit".

The Divine Messenger is generally known in Yoruba culture by the name *Eşu*. Among those who practice Yoruba religion in the west, the Divine Messenger is commonly known by the name *Elegba*. It is difficult to establish for certain how and why this shift in names occurred. However, it is known that in *Ifá* religion as it is practiced in Africa, *Elegba* is considered a warrior aspect of *Eşu*.

Elegba is a derivation of the term "*Ele Agbara*," which translates idiomatically to mean "The Power of Strength". As an aspect of *Eşu, Elegba* is the ability to communicate with Spirit in the face of overwhelming obstacles and oppression. Given the conditions that existed during slavery, it is not difficult to imagine why *Elegba* would become the primary focus of interaction between human consciousness and Spirit within *Ifá* worship as it exists in the west.

Eşu is considered one of many Spiritual Forces in Nature which are called "*Orisha*". The word *Orisha* means "Select Head". In a cultural context, *Orisha* is a reference to the various forces in Nature that guide consciousness. According to *Ifá*, everything in Nature has some form of consciousness called "*Orí*". The *Orí* of all animals, plants and humans is believed to be guided by a specific Force in Nature (*Orisha*) which defines the quality of a particular form of consciousness. There are a large number of *Orisha* and *each* Orisha has its own *awo*.

The unique function of Eşu within the realm of *Orisha Awo* (Mysteries of Nature) is to translate the language of humans into the language of Nature and to translate the language of Nature into the language of humans. The way in which this is done is the essence of the *awo* of *Eşu*.

Coconut Elegba for prayer and meditation

I.

ALO IRITÀN EŞU
FOLKTALES OF THE DIVINE MESSENGER

A. *LOJU-KOJU MEJI* — The Two Faces of the Divine Messenger

In the olden days there were two farmers who grew up together in a village located near the forest. As children they lived in the same compound sharing meals, playing games and learning the wisdom of their elders. They called each other "*Arákunrin*" which means "brother".

When the two young men reached the age of *akókò ti ọkunrin* (puberty), they were taken to *Ifá* for divination. On that day they were told that they would live their entire lives on adjacent farms. Because they were so close, their abundance depended on mutual cooperation. The *Babalawo* (diviner) told them that it was *Eşu* who would teach them the *awo ibaşepọ̀* (the mystery of cooperation), the *awo igbo* (the mystery of the forest) the *awo oko* (the mystery of farming), and the *awo 'fo aşẹ* (the mystery of invocation).

The *Babalawo* said that if they did not make regular *ebo* (offerings) to *EŞU*, the day would come when Eşu would pull them apart. If that day came, they would live their lives as enemies and suffer old age in poverty.

The two young men could not imagine being separated, they could not imagine being enemies and they could not imagine living their old age in poverty. Both of them thought that the *Babalawo* had been mistaken about their destiny. They saw no reason to make offerings to *Eşu*. They neglected the shrine to *Eşu* which stood at the entrance to their village. They assumed that their life of happiness would never change.

Some years later the two young men married and started to raise families. Together they had gone out into the forest and cleared a plot of land for a farm. Both farms were the same size, both farms grew the same crops and both men continued their friendship as they worked together tending the soil. One of the young men had learned from his father the techniques for pulling weeds and clearing brush. The other young man had learned from his father the techniques for drying seeds and watering the furrows. They depended on one another to insure that each years crop would provide enough food to feed their families with enough left over for trade at the market.

Both farms were separated by a narrow path that ran from the river to the village. The path was seldom used because there were no other fields in the area. Often the two men would work for weeks and even months without seeing anyone journey along the road that divided their land.

On the day that *Eşu* decided to travel down the path that ran between the two farms, *Eşu* remembered the words of the *Babalawo*. *Eşu* recognized the two farmers as the men who always passed his shrine at the entrance to the village without making an offering. Both young men continued to believe that they were skilled in the *awo oko* (mystery of farming). Between them they thought that they had all the ire (good fortune) they needed to create a good life. Life for each of them felt complete.

Eşu hid among the trees and watched the two men at work. As they bent over the earth, *Eşu* removed *efun* and *irosun* from his pouch. He took *ẹwẹ* (a large leaf) and mixed the *efun* with *omi tútù* (cool water), making *ọ̀da'fun* (white paint). He took another *ẹwẹ* (large leaf) and mixed the *irosun* with *oni tútù* (cool water), making *ọ̀da pon* (red paint). Using his fingers, *Eşu* painted the right side of his face *pon* (red) and the left side of his face *ofun* (white).

After placing the remaining *ọ̀da* (paint) back in his bag, *Eşu* walked down the path singing; "*Òro Eşu to to to akoni*," which means "The word of the Divine Messenger is always true".

As *Eşu* approached the two men who were working on their farm, they both looked up to see who was singing. *Eşu* was directly between them when they raised their heads. Using the index finger on each hand, *Eşu* drew their attention back to soil.

After *Eşu* disappeared from sight, *Arákunrin* on the right side of the road said; "Who was that strange man with *oju ofun* (the white face)?"

Arákunrin on the left side of the road answered; "Don't you mean the strange man with *ojú pon* (the red face)?"

Each question was asked in innocence, but the discussion soon led to a disagreement, the disagreement led to an argument and the argument led to a fight. Before the issue could be settled, both men were rolling on the ground tearing up their crops and destroying the ripe yams.

The damage to the farm caused a shortage of food, there were not enough yams left to feed their families and there was no surplus to take to the market. Each of the young men became so angered by what happened that they never spoke to each other again.

From that day on, those who praise *Eşu* always say; "*Eşu ma se mi o*," which means "Divine Messenger do not confuse me".

Commentary: The role of *Eşu* in *Orisha* worship is multi-dimensional. In this folktale, two friends have been advised by divination to make offerings to *Eşu* as a foundation for good fortune. They were told that *Eşu* would teach them the skills needed to be effective farmers, to make use of the natural elements in the forest and to learn the lessons needed to generate abundance. At this point, *Eşu* is presented in his role as Divine Messenger. In all *Ifá* ritual, *Eşu* is the link between the language of humans and the language of *Orisha*. *Ifá* ritual begins with an invocation to *Eşu* so that *Eşu* can direct the power of prayer to its intended recipient.

In most forms of occult science the ability to communicate between humans, Spirits and Forces in Nature is usually related to the powers of intuition that are generated by "The Third Eye". This idea is found in yogi tradition which identifies various power centers in the human body which are called "Chakras". *Ifá* also makes use of a system of chakras which it calls "*àwùję*". The *àwùję* that links human consciousness with *Orisha* consciousness is called "*ìwúję*". According to *Ifá*, the *ìwúję* is located in the central middle region of the forehead. This is slightly higher than the position associated with the third eye in yogi tradition.

When this power center is properly opened, impulses which enter the body from the outside world can be translated into intuitive impressions. The way this is done varies for different people. Intuition can take the form of strong feelings, visions, sounds and complex altered states in which the person experiences extraordinary dimensions of Being. During rituals of intitiation into the *awo* of *Orisha*, the *ìwúję* is opened through the use of herbal medicine that is applied directly to the forehead.

In this folktale the admonition to make offerings to *Eşu* is an instruction for the two friends to develop their powers of intuition so that they can communicate with the spirits of the forest. *Ifá* teaches that there are a wide variety of elemental spirits that maintain balance and order in the forest and under the earth. These Spirits come under a general grouping of Natural Forces called "*Ogboni*". The word *Ogboni* translates to mean "Of the Earth". The elemental spirits associated with *Ogboni* generate the consciousness of animals and plants. They usually do not come under the classification of Spirits known as *Orisha* because they do not manifest in personified form.

The advice from *Ifá* to the two friends was to maintain a respectful relationship with *Eşu* so that they could enhance their ability to communicate with those elemental spirits who would have a direct impact on the productivity of their farms.

In addition to the advice from the *Babalawo*, there is a warning. The two friends were told that if they do not make regular offerings to *Eşu*, the day will come when *Eşu* will pull them apart. This is a common warning in many of the folktales associated with *Eşu*. Frequently this is misinterpreted as an indication that *Eşu* is mean spirited or vicious. It would be more accurate to say that *Eşu* is functioning in his role as Divine Enforcer. Those who ignore issues of spiritual growth eventually suffer the consequences of their neglect.

The two friends believe that nothing could pull them apart. They thought that all they needed was each other's friendship to survive in the world. The folktale is making a very clear statement that those who live in Nature must respect the ways of Nature in order to take advantage of Nature's blessings. By ignoring their relationship to *Eşu*, the two men are resisting any communication from the elemental spirits who maintain ecological balance in the forest and on the farm. It is possible to temporarily disrespect the Laws of Nature, but such disregard always comes with a price.

If you pollute the water in the river, the water will eventually become undrinkable. If you deplete the soil on the farm, eventually plants will not grow. If you destroy large segments of the rain forest, the effects on climate and air density can disrupt the fertility of large sections of the earth. When anyone disregards Natural Law for an extended period of time, Nature has a way of reacting in the interest of self-preservation. Such reactions as drought and famine can seem disruptive and harsh. However, from a metaphysical perspective natural disasters can be understood as attempts by the Forces of Nature to communicate fundamental information regarding the dynamics of Being.

In *Ifá* scripture it is generally *Eşu* who carries this type of message from Nature to humans. When *Eşu* is carrying a warning from Spirit, *Eşu* assumes the role of Trickster. There is nothing demonic or sinister about the Spiritual role of Trickster in any Earth-centered religion. The function of the Tricksters is always to force human consciousness into a deeper understanding of self and world.

In this instance, *Eşu* paints one side of his face white and the other side of his face red. The argument between the two former friends is rooted in the truth of their own limited perspective. Each of the men considers himself to be right and the other to be wrong. At the heart of their dispute is the inability to consider the possibility that they both might be right. The world described in *Ifá* myth is seldom a world of either/or. In most instances it is a world of both/and. What this means is that consciousness is a constantly shifting reality. Information which may be true for one person on a given day, may have no value for someone else in a different circumstance. The shifting value of objective information can only be evaluated from a broad perspective and it is *Eşu* who plays a key role in providing that perspective.

When humans become too set in their ways, too rigid in their thinking and too dogmatic in their response to other points of view, it is *Eşu* who stirs up the mix and forces the kind of re-evaluation that can lead to enlightenment.

In this story the disruption caused by *Eşu* does not lead to enlightenment. Instead it leads to an argument, loss of friendship and poverty. The point here is that Nature will always respond to those who are in need of spiritual transformation, but not everyone who is blessed with instruction from *Eşu* will grasp the meaning of the lesson that is to be learned. Within the context of *Ifá*, every disruption is considered an opportunity for learning and growth.

Spiritual transformation always contains an element of choice, an element of freewill and an element of responsibility. Those who are unwilling to embrace these qualities project their weakness onto the world and claim that *Eşu* is a demon. *Ifá* scripture is very clear that demons are not Spiritual Forces generated by Creation. Demons are human inventions created and invoked by those who resist living in harmony with Nature.

B. *Ọ̀BE EŞU* — the Divine Messenger's Knife

Ajá consulted *Ifá* on the day that he wanted a wife. He was told to take an *ọ̀bẹ* (knife) to *ojà* (the market) and use it to make *ebo* (offerings) to *Eşu*. When he arrived in *ojà* (the market), *Ajá* stopped to buy *iyán* (pounded yams) from *Omo'lorí* (the daughter of the chief). As he reached for the *iyán* (yams), *Eşu* pushed him from behind and he accidently cut the *Omo'lorí's* hand.

The *Awon Agbagba* (elders) of *ojà* (the market) demanded *onídajó* (justice). *Eşu* spoke on behalf of *Ajá* and said that it was an accident. To settle the dispute, *Eşu* suggested that *Ajá* take care of *Omo'lorí* until her hand healed. *Ajá* agreed. While *Ajá* took care of *Omo'lorí* she agreed to become his wife.

Commentary: In this story the main character is called "*Ajá*" which means "dog". In *Ifá* mythology the dog is sacred to *Ogun*. Whenever a character appears in a Yoruba folktale with the name of an animal associated with a particular *Orisha*, it is assumed that the character is an aspect of that *Orisha. Ogun* is the Spirit of Iron and is associated with the trade of blacksmith.

Ajá is instructed by *Ifá* to carry a knife to the shrine of *Eşu.* Because the knife is sacred to *Ogun*, the story is making a symbolic reference to the *awo* of *Ogun. Eşu* is telling *Ajá* to take the power of his *Orisha* with him in search of a wife. In the process of making the offering *Ajá* encounters an accidental series of circumstances that leads to his marriage. It is the very act of appealing to *Orisha* that creates the desired result.

In the previous story *Eşu* caused disruption among two friends who refused to make offerings to *Orisha* with disastrous results. In this story *Eşu* causes disruption for someone who has agreed to make offerings to *Orisha* with positive results.

The suggestion here is that good intentions will bring blessings even in the midst of difficulty.

Consecrated Eşu

II.

ÌMỌ̀ EṢU
THE THEOLOGICAL FUNCTION OF THE DIVINE MESSENGER

A. *EṢU ÀYÀNMỌ́-ÌPIN* — The Divine Messenger and The Concept of Destiny

The *Ifá* concept of "*àyànmọ́-ipin,*" which means "Destiny," is based on the belief that each person chooses their individual destiny before being born into the world. These choices materialize as those components that form human potential. Within the scope of each person's potential there exists parameters of choice that can enhance or inhibit the fullest expression of individual destiny. *Ifá* calls these possibilities "*ọ̀na ipin,*" which means "fate lines". Each decision that is made in the course of one life time can effect the range of possibilities that exists in the future, by either limiting or expanding the options for growth.

It is within the context of choice or what is known in western philosophical tradition as "free will" that *Eṣu* has an important function. Each moment of existence includes a wide range of possible actions, reactions and interpretations. Those moments which require decisive action are described in *Ifá* scripture as "*ọ̀na'padẹ̀*" which means "junction in the road". Whenever a person who is trying to build character through the use of *Ifá* spiritual discipline reaches *ọ̀na'padẹ̀*, it is customary to consult *Eṣu* regarding the question of which path will bring blessings from *Orisha.*

Ifá teaches that blessings come to those who make choices that are consistent with their highest destiny. Within Yoruba culture it is understood that an individual's highest destiny is based on those choices that build "*ìwa-pẹ̀lẹ́*," which means "good character".

B. *EȘU NI BA KO* — The Divine Messenger as the Source of Deception

The discipline of *Ifá* includes training in the use of various forms of altered consciousness. In Yoruba altered states of consciousness are called "*Ìfáiyà*" and they are used to engage in communication with *Orisha*. *Ìfáiyà* includes "*ogbón inú*," which is heightened intuition "*ìsotélè*," which is the ability to see into the future "*alála*," which is communication with *Orisha* through dreams; "*Egúngun*," which is possession by an ancestor spirit; and "*Orisha'gun*" which is possession by a Force in Nature.

Training in these skills requires the ability to distinguish between "*ọfọ Orisha*" which is "the voice of Spirit," and "*ọfọ egun*," which is "the voice of the ancestors," and "*Eșu ni ba ko*" which is what would be described in western terminology as the projection of personal fantasy. When someone is beginning the process of communication with either *Orisha* or *egun*, the manifestation of that communication is often very similar in form to daydreaming or fantasy. By opening certain power centers in the *orí* it is possible to have visions that are influenced by external forces. The ability to interpret these visions is at the heart of *Orisha awo* (Mysteries of Nature).

When someone identifies personal projection as *ọfọ Orisha*, *Ifá* describes this condition as "*Eșu ni ba ko*". In the west this phrase is frequently translated to mean "The Divine Messenger is a Trickster". A literal translation would be "The Divine Messenger is not Spirit". This does not mean that *Eșu* is seen as something less than an *Orisha*. It suggests that *Eșu* in his role as trickster can generate altered states of consciousness in which self-deception is confused with either *ọfọ Orisha* (The Voice of Nature) or *ọfọ egun* (The voice of the ancestors).

According to *Ifá* spiritual practice, the seat of self-deception is the back of the neck where the skull meets the spine. It is at this point that the emotions generated by the power center at the heart link with the thoughts generated by the power centers in the head. Those who block their emotions or who refuse to integrate the head and the heart create a condition which is described in *Ifá* as *Eşu ni ba ko*.

The area at the base of the skull on the back of the neck is one of the key places to receive spiritual cleansings whenever a person is out of alignment with their destiny. The back of the neck is sometimes referred to as "*Ilę Eşu ni ba ko*," which means "The house of the Divine Trickster".

C. *ÒGBÓ EŞU* — The Staff of the Divine Messenger

In Africa the wooden statues that are used to represent *Eşu* frequently show him carrying an "*ògbó*," which means "cudgel". This staff is also called "*Ilari*," which means "enlightenment of consciousness". The word *Ilari* is used to describe the staff carried by the messengers of the *Oba* (Regional Chief).

By tradition, the *Ilari* gives *Eşu* the ability to transcend the physical restrictions of time and space. In the terminology of western physics, the *Ilari* symbolizes *Eşu's* ability to function in the fourth dimension. This means that messages from *Eşu* are able to travel great distances in an instant and that he is able to appear and disappear at will. In a sense the *Ilari* represents all forms of psychic phenomena that defy western theories of cause and effect.

Those western scientists who dismiss all forms of spirit communication because they do not conform to physical science seem to be missing the point. *Ifá* teaches that *Eşu's* function in ritual is to make connection with those Forces in Nature that do manifest openly to the realm of the senses.

D. *EŞU ONITOJU AŞĘ* — The Divine Messenger as the Source of Spiritual Power

Ifá cosmology is based on the belief that the Primal Source of Creation is a form of Spiritual Essence called "*aşę*". There is no literal translation for *aşę*, although it is used in prayer to mean "May it be so".

Ifá teaches that the visible universe is generated by two dynamic forces. One is the force of "*inàlọ*," which means "expansion," and the other is the force of "*isọki*," which means "contraction". The first initial manifestation of these forces is through "*ìmọ*," which means "light," and through "*aimoyé*," which means "darkness". In *Ifá* myth expansion and light are identified with Male Spirits called "*Orisha'ko*". Contraction and darkness are identified with Female Spirits called "*Orisha'bo*". Neither manifestation of *aṣẹ* is considered superior to the other and both are viewed as essential elements in the overall balance of Nature.

In *Ifá* cosmology both *ìmọ* and *aimoyé* arise from the matrix of the invisible universe which is called "*imolẹ*," which means "house of light". Within the house of light there is an invisible substance that transforms spiritual potential into physical reality. The invisible substance that moves between these two dimensions is called *aṣẹ*, and it is *Eṣu* who is given the task of guiding the distribution of *aṣẹ* throughout Creation.

Western science teaches that matter and energy are neither created or destroyed, they simply become transformed. *Ifá* teaches that it is *Eṣu* who guides this process of transformation. It is the *awo* of this particular role of *Eṣu* that associated him with the principle of Divine Justice.

III.

ỌNA EṢU
THE ROADS OF THE DIVINE MESSENGER

Eşu has clear functions as Messenger, Trickster and Enforcer of Divine Justice. However, the way that each of these functions becomes manifest is dependant upon the various aspects of *Eşu*. These aspects are usually called "*Ọ̀na Eşu*," which means "Roads of The Divine Messenger". Generally *Ifá* describes *Eşu* as having twenty-one roads. In most cases, these roads describe the appearance of *Eşu* in *Odu* which are the sacred scripture of *Ifá*. But because there is a wide range of variation in Africa with regard to the content of *Odu*, and there are some regional differences in the descriptions of *Ọ̀na Eşu*.

The Roads of The Divine Messenger that are presented here are the aspects of *Eşu* as they are in *Ègbẹ̀ Ifá*, Ode Remo, which is located in Ogun State in the southwestern region of Nigeria.

A. *EŞU ORO*

Eşu Oro is the Divine Messenger of the Power of the Word. This aspect of *Eşu* is related to the ability of the spoken word to create spiritual transformation through the use of incantations. Certain words that are used in *Ifá* and *Orisha* ritual have no literal translation. They are used because the contain tonal qualities that resonate with particular Forces of Nature. The power of resonation is the ability to create tonal vibrations that are similar to those frequencies generated by specific *Orisha*. When a similar frequency is established it has the power of attraction. In Western Occult terminology this is called "sympathetic magic".

B. *EŞU OPIN*

Eşu Opin is the Divine Messenger of Boundaries. In *Ifá* ritual boundaries are marked to establish sacred space. Frequently the space that is to be used for ritual purposes is marked with a mat. In many Yoruba homes, the space reserved for the *Orisha* is a small room attached to the house that is used exclusively for ceremonial work. *Ifá* also makes use of sacred groves called "*Igbodu*". These groves have clearly defined boundaries which are off limits to the initiated. Whenever sacred space is established there is almost always some manifestation of *Eşu* present as the guardian of the ritual boundaries.

When *Eşu Opin* is placed at a sacred site, it also has the function of keeping that area charged with *aşẹ*, which *Ifá* identifies as the primal source of transformation in Creation.

C. *EŞU ALAKETU*

Eşu Alaketu is the Divine Messenger of the City of *Ketu*. The prefix "ala" refers to "light" or "Divine guidance". In most instances *Eşu Alaketu* is associated with the *Orisha Oshun* who is the Spirit of Fresh Water, Sensuality and Abundance. The city of *Alaketu* is located near the city of *Oşogbo*, which is the location of the primary *Oshun* Shrine within *Ifá* religion. The myth associated with *Eşu* in the city of *Alaketu* refers to the great power of *Eşu* and *Oshun* to transform that which has decayed. The decay referred to in the myth is ethical decay. The power of *Eşu Alaketu* is the ability to invoke the sacred use of sensuality can be used to elevate moral degeneration.

D. *EŞU ISẸRI*

Eşu Isẹri is the Divine Messenger of the Morning Dew. *Ifá* makes extensive use of herbs as both medicine for physical healing and medicine for spiritual healing. The wisdom of herbs generally comes under the influence of the *Orisha Osanyin* (The Spirit of Medicine). The initiates into the mysteries of *Osanyin* make extensive use of prayer and ritual in the planting, picking and preparation of herb medicine. In many instances the best time to pick herbs that grew in the forest is just before sun rise. It is a time when dew lingers on the leaves adding another source of power to their inherent qualities.

Many words in Yoruba have multiple meanings depending on the context. The word "*Isçri*" means "morning dew;" however it is also a contraction of "*isç*" and "*orí*" which means "deeds of the head". In *Eşu's* role as Divine Enforcer deeds of the head are recorded as basis for maintaining Divine Justice in the process of *atunwa* (reincarnation).

E. *EŞU GOGO*

Eşu Gogo is the Divine Messenger of Full Payment. This is one of the aspects of *Eşu* that has the function of enforcing Divine Justice. The payment spoken of here is not limited to money or the exchange of goods. Payment includes the metaphysical consequences of foolish and unjust behavior. In some ways the idea of full payment is similar to the Buddhist idea of Karma. All actions have consequences, including an effect on the process of *atunwa* (reincarnation).

This aspect of *Eşu* is generally associated with swift, sharp and precise action as it relates to the termination of a conflict or issues involving confusion and misunderstanding. The ability of *Eşu* to function in the fourth dimension gives him the ability to cause transformation which is generated outside the physical dimensions of time and space.

F. *EŞU WARA*

Eşu Wara is the Divine Messenger of Personal Relationships. *Ifá* teaches that each person comes to the world with a specific Destiny. Each Destiny has lines of inter-section and inter-action with the Destiny of those we come in contact with throughout our lives. In traditional Yoruba culture there is a strong emphasis on maintaining the structure of the family and of honoring the relationships that exist in an extended family. Whenever two people are considering some form of long term relationship they frequently consult with a diviner to determine the parameters of a given relationship. This is true for both intimate relationships and those relationships that would be considered more formal.

Because of the subject element that is prevalent in most personal relationships, *Eşu Wara* is frequently associated with the power of confusion.

G. *EŞU IJẸLU*

Eşu Ijẹlu is the Divine Messenger of the Drum. In *Ifá* ritual the drums have a key role as part of the invocation process. The *dundun* drum in particular is able to mimic the sounds of the Yoruba language and is used as a tool for calling specific spirits to a given ceremony. The word "*Ijẹlu*" means "Feeder of the Drum". Most drums that are used in *Ifá* and *Orisha* ritual are sanctified through the use of offerings that are presently directly the drum. It is *Eşu Ijẹlu* who guides this feeding process.

H. *EŞU AIYEDẸ*

Eşu Aiyedẹ is the Divine Messenger who arrives on Earth. In *Ifá* Scripture references to *Eşu* making the journey from Heaven to Earth are references to messages sent from Spirit to humans. Frequently these messages may not be in response to prayer, but come from Spirit in the form of mystic and prophetic vision. These visions are believed to provide guidance beyond the limited concerns of normal everyday consciousness.

I. *EŞU ÒDÀRÀ*

Eşu Òdàrà is the Divine Messenger of Transformation. This aspect of *Eşu* is closely associated with *Ifá*. All *Ifá* initiates receive *Eşu Òdàrà* as a part of "*Tefá*," which is the Yoruba word for "*Ifá* initiation". The reason for this is because *Ifá* priests are the guardians of the vast spectrum of *Awo* (Mysteries) associated with spiritual growth and transformation. These Mysteries are preserved in the *Odu* (scripture) that are used as the basis for *Ifá* divination. Whenever *Ifá* divination is performed, *Eşu Òdàrà* is generally one of the first Spirits that is invoked.

In *Ifá* and *Orisha*, ritual transformation is associated with the element of fire. When *Eşu Òdàrà* is feed, it is common to use burning palm oil to raise the *aşẹ* (spiritual power) needed to invoke spiritual growth.

J. *EŞU JEKI EBO DA*

Eşu Jeki Ebo Da is the Divine Messenger who sanctions Life Force Offerings. In Africa many shrines and even homes have a place that is used for the slaughtering of animals that are being prepared for food. Many of the rituals associated with *Ifá* involve a communal meal. This requires that the meat be prepared in a sacred manner. *Eşu Jeki Ebo Da* is associated with this process.

The media has tended to unfamiliarly characterize Life Force Offerings as "animal sacrifice". The term animal sacrifice suggests tends to suggest that animals are cruelly treated then discarded. That is not what occurs in Africa. Food is prepared in much the same way that Kosher food by Rabbis.

K. *EŞU AGONGON GOJA*

Eşu Agongon Goja is the Divine Messenger of the Wide Belt. In this context a wide belt refers to one of the *Awo* (Mysteries) associated with the clothing that is used for ceremonial work. Clothing used in rituals for *Ifá, Orisha* and *Egun* have both a symbolic function and a protective function. The way a person dresses for a particular ritual will have the effect of drawing certain Spiritual Forces to them while repelling others.

L. *EŞU ELEKUN*

Eşu Elekun is one of the Divine Messengers associated with hunters and warriors. The word "*Elekun*" means "Leapard". In

Yoruba culture the leapard is a symbol of strength, cunning and courage. These are traits generally associated with *Ogun* (The Spirit of Iron). It is priests of *Ogun* who usually guide young men through the rites of passage that occur at puberty. These rites of passage include a test of courage that prepares young men for their social roles as defenders of the family and community.

M. *EŞU AROWOJẸ*

Eşu Arowoje is the Divine Messenger for those who travel the ocean. This *Eşu* is associated with the Spirit of the Ocean which is called; "*Olokun*" in Africa. The word "*arowoje*" refers to the shore of the ocean. It is at the shoreline that the Natural Forces of earth and water intermingle. It is *Eşu Arowoję* who guides this interaction.

N. *EŞU LALU*

Eşu Lalu is the Divine Messenger of Dance. In *Ifá* ritual the use of dance is one of the methods for inducing those altered states that result in direct communication with *Orisha*. The process of Spirit communication involves the absorption of energy called; "*aşę*" from the environment into the body. Dances used for specific *Orisha* have the function of opening specific power centers in the body that are closely attuned to a particular *Orisha*. *Eşu* has the task of assisting in the guidance of this process.

O. *EŞU PAKUTA SI EWA*

Eşu Pakuta Si Ewa is the Divine Messenger who creates and destroys beauty. *Ifá* teaches that all things that come into Being in the World go through a cycle of birth, growth, death and rebirth. This process of transformation includes the destruction of that which is considered beautiful and harmonious. Such destruction creates a foundation for the re-birth of that which is to come.

P. *EŞU KẸWẸ LẸ DUNJẸ*

Eşu Kẹwẹ Lẹ Dunjẹ is the Divine Messenger who eats sweets. The use of sweet tasting food in both *Ifá* ritual and medicine has the function of counter-balancing the bitterness which can make life seem harsh and burdensome. *Ifá* scripture is clear that sweetness has a much needed place in daily life as a source of inspiration and joy.

Giving *Eşu* sweets is frequently used as a method for invoking abundance. In *Ifá* abundance includes wealth, long life and children.

Q. *EŞU ELEBARA*

Eşu Elegbara is the Divine Messenger of Power. The power that is spoken of here is the power of the warrior. Not all warrior power is directed towards power. It is the type of tireless persistence that sees a task done to completion. At times this power is clearly associated with issues of personal and communal protection. In the west this aspect of *Eşu* has become known as *Elegba.*

R. *EŞU EMALONA*

Eşu Emalona is the Divine Messenger of any means. *Ifá* is a tradition that is based on the development of character which in turn is based on a very clear set of cultural expectations. But *Ifá* also recognizes the reality that at times special circumstances require extra-ordinary measures. The more forceful aspects of *Eşu* are always invoked with clear guidance from *Orisha* as it is expressed through divination. Those who use force based on personal motivation alone frequently find themselves in violation of both communal and spiritual taboo.

The word "*emalona*" means "the fifth road." It is a reference to the gateway into the invisible dimension.

S. *EŞU LAROYẸ*

Eşu Laroyẹ is the Divine Messenger of *Oshun* (The River Goddess) in her role as guardian of the *Awo* (Mysteries) of *Ìwa ifẹkufẹ* (sensuality) and *Letu loju* (fertility). The word "*laroyẹ*" is loosely translated to mean "close to the mothers". It is one of the praise names used to invoke *Oshun.*

T. *EŞU ANANAKI*

Eşu Ananaki is the Divine Messenger of the past. *Ifá* teaches that we become who we are by standing on the shoulders of those who have come before us. We progress by remembering both the deeds of our ancestors and by remembering the lessons that are brought to earth directly through the intervention of Natural Forces or *Orisha.*

U. *EŞU OKOBURU*

Eşu Okoburu is the Divine Enforcer. The word "*okoburu*" means "wicked cudgel". This does not mean that it is a weapon used by "evil" people. It suggests that it is a weapon used to punish injustice.

IV.

OJUBO IBORA
THE SHRINE OF THE DIVINE MESSENGER

A. *OJUBO IBORA ADURA* — Shrine for Prayer and Meditation

In traditional Yoruba homes the shrine for *Eşu* is usually outside near the place where animals are prepared for cooking. Many villages have a communal shrine for *Eşu* that is located either near the entrance to the town or near the entrance to the market. Also most *Igbodu* have some aspect of *Eşu* located within the boundaries of the sacred grove.

The art of making a consecrated *Eşu* is very complicated and within the traditions of *Ifá* and *Orisha* the task of making an *Eşu* belongs to those who have been initiated into the priesthood. For those who do not have access to elders of either *Ifá* or *Orisha*, it is possible to set up a shrine for *Eşu* that is used as a focal point for prayer and meditation. Such should not be used for the invocation of *Eşu*. The difference is that the use of prayer and meditation is a way of respecting the power of *Eşu*, while invocation is the process of making use of *Eşu's* power. Invocation is limited to those who receive a fully consecrated *Eşu* from an elder.

For those who want to build a shrine for *Eşu* that can be used for meditation and prayer, start by purchasing a coconut. Every coconut has three small circles on one side. These circles often resemble two eyes and a mouth. They form what is called the face of the coconut. Be sure to select a coconut with a face that is both clear and appealing. Some stores cover the surface of the coconut with wax, so it might be necessary to remove the wax with a knife.

Select a place either inside or outside your home that will be used as a shrine for *Eşu*. If the shrine is to go inside the house it is traditional to place a mat near the front door. If the shrine is to go outside it is traditional to build a small house for the shrine which provides a roof and four walls with a door that can be locked. Such a house can be two feet square or smaller depending on space.

When you have selected the place where the shrine is to be seated, place the coconut near the spot along with a bowl of water, a candle and either palm oil or protection oil. Light the candle, then clean the surface of the coconut. At this point you will say a simple prayer which is not an invocation. The prayer is as follows:

Iba a sę Eşu.
I respect the Spirit of the Divine Messenger.
Iba a sę Eşu.
I respect the Spirit of the Divine Messenger.
Iba a sę Eşu.
I respect the Spirit of the Divine Messenger.
Aşę.
May it be so.

Now sit with the coconut and ask *Eşu* to reveal the form that is best suited to the work that you need to do. You may feel that the coconut by itself is adequate, or you may feel that it needs to be painted. Traditionally the colors associated with *Eşu* are either black and red or black and white. Continue sitting with the coconut until you see the colors that are to be used and the types of images that should go on the face. Once this is clear, paint the image on the coconut.

I recommend that once the face is painted that it be placed in a basket filled with dirt. The dirt should be from either a sacred site or from your favorite place in nature. When the paint has dried rub either the palm oil or the protection oil over the surface of the coconut. While you are doing this ask *Eşu* to protect your house and to place you firmly on the path of spiritual growth and transformation.

Whenever a prayer is made it is appropriate to make an offering. The coconut representation of *Eşu* can be given a few drops of rum, popcorn and candy.

B. *OJUBO IBORA ORIKI* — Shrine for Invocation

When a person is given *Eşu* by either an initiate of *Ifá* or *Orisha*, the *Eşu* is generally presented in association with *Osun, Ogun* and *Ochosi*. Together these four Spiritual Forces are part of a grouping of Spirits called "*Ibora*". The *Ibora* are considered to be Spirits that have a responsibility to protect those who are the path of building character and of spiritual transformation.

The symbolic representation for *Eşu* is either a rock, a small face or a carved statue of a man carrying a cudgel wearing a long flowing cap. The methods for making *Eşu* are considered "*ohun ìkoko,*" which means "secret". Most aspects of *ohun ikoko* are taught orally, and passed from teacher to student through direct transmission. In Ode Remo those who care for the consecrated shrines of *Eşu* invoke the Spirit of *Eşu* at the shrine on either a five day, or a sixteen day cycle. The reason that invocations are said on a regular basis is because *Ifá* teaches that the power of *Orisha* only remains in a given place for as long as it is called to that place.

There is a complex collection of prayers and invocations that are used by those who are initiated into *Ifá* and *Orisha*. Many of these prayers are used for specific seasonal celebrations or for specific rituals of transformation. Prayers that are used for invocation of *Orisha* are generally called "*Oriki*". Most *Oriki* tend to follow a certain format that allows for some variation depending on the circumstances. The format is as follows:

a. Begin the invocation of *Eşu* by stating your own name.

Mo ni (your name).
I am (your name).

b. If you are either an *Ifá* or *Orisha* initiate begin by stating the name that was given to you during *Igbodu*.

Mo te de (your title).
I have become (your title).

c. Following the introduction comes the call to *Eşu* which includes a recitation of praise names. These praise names come under the general heading of *Oroko Iyin* and include words with the proper tonal qualities for invocation which do not necessarily have a literal translation. Names may be chosen from the following praises:

Òkàràmàhó

Ayànràkàtá – awo –'lẹ̀ – ojà

Òyìnsèsẹ̀

Sègûri-Alàgbàjá

Amónisẹ̀gùn-mapo

d. After *Eşu* has been called by his praise names, it is customary to call him by some of the descriptive praises that describe his power. Among the praise names that may be used are the following:

Eşu lanlu ogirioko.
Divine Messenger speak with power.
Okunrin orí ita.
Man of the crossroads.
Onimini nf'ìmu mi Eşu n fi.
I respect the Spirit of the Divine Messenger with all of my soul.
Torí ẹni Eşu ba nşẹ ki ìmo.
The Divine Messenger is the first one who I praise.
Alayiki a juba.
I respect the one we salute by dancing in a circle.

e. Following the use of the qualities of the Divine Messenger comes the actual call or invocation. Each part of the call is generally repeated three times for emphasis:

Eşu o pẹ o
Divine Messenger I greet you.
Eşu o pẹ o.
Divine Messenger I greet you.
Eşu o pẹ o.
Divine Messenger I greet you.
Eşu pẹ̀lẹ́ o.
Divine Messenger I am greeting you.
Eşu pẹ̀lẹ́ o.
Divine Messenger I am greeting you.
Eşu pẹ̀lẹ́ o.
Divine Messenger I am greeting you.

f. When the invocation is completed make a offering directly to The Divine Messenger:

Eşu jẹun (identify the offering), ***a dupẹ.***
Divine Messenger eat my offering of (identify the offering). I thank you.

g. After the offering has been made, make either prayers of praise or a request for assistance. Some forms of praise are as follows:

Oro Eşu to to to akoni.
The word of the Divine Messenger is always respected.
Eşu orí mi ma jẹ nko o.
The Divine Messenger guides my head on the path of transformation.
Eşu ohun ni'ma wa kiri.
The Divine Messenger has the voice that roams the universe.
Eşu ma sẹ me o.
Divine Messenger do not confuse me.

V.

EȘU OLOTOJU ENU ONA ORUN

THE DIVINE MESSENGER AS GATEKEEPER TO THE INVISIBLE REALM

The *Ifá* symbol of Creation is a circle that has been divided into four quadrants by an equal arm cross. The top half of the circle represents *Ikolẹ Orun* which is the Invisible Realm of Spiritual influence and the primal source of Creation. The bottom half of the tray represents *Ikolẹ Ayẹ* which is the visible dimensions of Earth. The right side of the tray, both top and bottom, represent *àyànmọ́-ipin* which is Destiny or the future. The left side of the tray, both top and bottom, represents *iwẹ itan* which is the past.

Ifá teaches that all of these dimensions influence and literally create each new moment in time. The center of the circle at the juncture of both arms of the cross represents *Ita Orun* which is the pathway to the Invisible Realm. According to *Ifá* the only way to receive the blessing of Creation is to live life in balance and harmony with all those Forces that Create the Circle of Creation. Symbolically this occurs by standing at the center of the Circle is a state of harmony with all those aspects of reality that produce time as it exists in the present. Standing on the road of *Ita Orun* is believed to produce "*ìwa-pẹ̀lẹ́*," which means "good character". The doorway to *Ita Orun* is called "*olotoju enuouna Orun*," which means "owner of the mouth of the road to Source". It is *Eşu* in all of his manifestations who is the guardian of this gateway, which is why all rituals in *Ifá* and *Orisha* worship begin and end with prayers to *Eşu*.

VI.

ORIN EŞU

SONGS TO THE DIVINE MESSENGER

A. Call: ***Ibara'go ago mo juba, Ibara'go ago mo juba, omo de ko ri koyi, ibara'go mo juba, Elegba Eşu lona.***
(Divine Trickster I salute you, I salute you by giving thanks, Divine Trickster I salute you, I salute you by giving thanks, children rise, do not become drowned in misfortune, Owner of Power, Divine Messenger of the Road)
Response: Repeat.
Call: ***Ishon shon abe ishon shon abe Odara kolorire eyo baba se mi.***
(The point of the knife, the point of the knife, Spirit of Transformation do not bring misfortune, instead use your medicine to save me).
Response: ***Ishon shon abe.***
(The point of your knife).
Call: ***Odara koloriri eyo baba semi.***
(Spirit of Transformation do not bring misfortune, instead use your medicine to save me).
Response: ***Ishon shon abe.***
(The point of the knife).
Call: ***Odara kolorire eyo.***
(Spirit of Transformation do not bring misfortune).
Response: ***Ishon shon abe ishon shon abe Odara kolorire eyo baba semi ishon shon abe.***
(The point of the knife, the point of the knife, Spirit of Transformation do not bring misfortune, instead use your medicine to save me).

B. Call: ***Iba Orisha iba la yeo ase mo juba.***
(I respect the Immortals, I respect the power of Spirit and we give praise).
Response: Iba Orisha iba la yeo.

(I respect the Immortals, I respect the power of Spirit).
Call: ***Aloro mo juba.***
(For pure words we give praise).
Response: ***Iba Orisha iba la yeo.***
(I respect the Immortals, I respect the power of Spirit).
Call: ***Iworo mo juba.***
(For good word we give praise).
Response: ***Iba Orisha iba la yeo.***
(I respect the Immortals and I respect the power of Spirit).
Call: ***Ase mo juba Orisha mo juba mo juba Orisha.***
(May it be so, we give praise to the Immortals, we give praise, we give praise to the Immortals).
Response: ***Ase mo juba Orisha.***
(May it be so, we give praise to the Immortals).
Call ***Mo juba ile mo juba Orisha.***
(We give praise to the house of the Immortals).
Response ***Ase mo juba Orisha.***
(May it be so we give praise to the Immortals).
Call: ***Mo juba, mo juba Orisha.***
(May it be so, we give praise to the Immortals).
Response: ***Ase mo juba Orisha.***
(May it be so, we give praise to the Immortals).

C. Call ***Obara waiyo, eke, Eşu Odara, omo yana wana mama ke iyawo e.***
(Spirit of Transformation come to earth twice, Spirit of Transformation, child who does not deviate from favor with the mothers).
Response: Repeat.
Call: ***Edi wo, edi wo ago meta meta.***
(Creator of abundance, creator of abundance we call you three times).
Response: ***Edi wo, edi wo ago meta meta oti mole le seka.***
Creator of abundance, creator of abundance we call you three times and the power of light).

Item #005
$14.95

POWERS OF THE ORISHAS

Santeria and the Worship of Saints

Migene Gonzalez Wippler

Santeria is the Afro-Cuban religion based on an amalgamation between some of the magio-religious beliefs and practices of the Yoruba people and those of the Catholic church. In Cuba where the Yoruba proliferated extensively, they became known as *Lucumi,* a word that means "friendship".

Santeria is known in Cuba as Lucumi Religion. The original Yoruba language, interspersed with Spanish terms and corrupted through the centuries of misuse and mispronunciation, also became known as Lucumi. Today some of the terms used in Santeria would not be recognized as Yoruba in Southwestern Nigeria, the country of origin of the Yoruba people.

Santeria is a Spanish term that means a confluence of saints and their worship. These saints are in reality clever disguises for some of the Yoruba deities, known as Orishas. During the slave trade, the Yoruba who were brought to Cuba were forbidden the practice of their religion by their Spanish masters. In order to continue their magical and religious observances safely the slaves opted for the identification and disguise of the Orishas with some of the Catholic saints worshipped by the Spaniards. In this manner they were able to worship their deities under the very noses of the Spaniards without danger of punishment.

ISBN 0-942272-25-0 5½"x 8½" 144 pages $14.95

Toll Free: 1 (888) OCCULT - 1
www.OCCULT1.com

MORE BOOKS FROM ORIGINAL PUBLICATIONS

SECRETS OF THE PSALMS
$11.95

8,9,10 BOOKS OF MOSES
$10.95

PSALM WORKBOOK
$14.95

THE BOOK ON PALO
$21.95

COMPLETE BK OF VOODOO
$19.95

COMPLETE BOOK OF BATHS
$9.95

SPIRITUAL CLEANSING
$9.95

PAPA JIM HERB MAGIC
$9.95

LOTTERY # DREAMBOOK
$14.95